SHAPESHIFTING

HEATHER STEWART

GOLDEN
BRIDGES

SHAPESHIFTING

GOLDEN
BRIDGES
PUBLISHING

Published in the United States by Golden Bridges Publishing 2024

Library of Congress Control Number:

ISBN (Print): 979-8-9907356-6-8

ISBN (ebook): 979-8-9907356-7-5

CONTENTS

PART TWO
SHELLBACK

PART THREE
MERMAID

To my fellow women in service

Who have also been

Mothers

Aunties

Daughters

Nieces

Monstresses

And

Goddesses

PUBLISHER'S NOTE

This book is a poetic memoir written by one individual based on her own interpretation of experiences. It represents the personal views and opinions of the author and does not necessarily reflect the positions or opinions of any organization, institution, or individual with which the author is affiliated, included, but not limited to the United States Navy. The content presented herein is based on the author's perspective and interpretation of the subject matter. Neither the publisher nor any associated parties shall be held responsible for any consequences arising from the opinions or interpretations expressed within this book.

PART ONE
POLLYWOG

a newly formed, uninitiated sea creature
still searching the seas
for quests that may lead to greatness

ONCE UPON A SHORE

Sitting by the open sea, I sat to ponder life to be

Sat and wondered, thinking many things

For out there, somewhere, lived the wanderers

And out there, somewhere, wonder waits for them

There where the wanderers met wondrous things

That was where I really longed to be, to live,

Then upon my pondering dream, I saw it

All tentacles and whispering, there it was, it'd come to me

When it spoke, it whispered things

I had always wished to hear

From across the sea it promised me I'd find

These very things I'd pondered here,

Never thinking I could even try to strive for them

For it was all too much, too far to try for

With not so much as a map to guide me

So, I set upon the time next day to say goodbye to them

For all those sights I knew I'd miss one day

For now was the time to take to miss them all

To leap and go and see, to sit upon the shore no more

But to make my way across the sea

SEAPUP

a recent graduate of boot camp
Ignorant in the ways of the seafaring world
with a glorious lack of common sense
Who is much in need of guidance
Synonyms – boot; shower shoe

SEAMOM

a crone upon a vessel
usually guiding children away from the furnace
sometimes working deals with the sea witch;
can be found crafting escape hatches

HOW TO BEGIN

The first step is so easy that it's not even ours to take

It begins with a simple invitation

A conversation with some people who convince so smoothly

That you hardly realize that you're signing up

For things that are explained and somehow not at all

Then there comes a hotel and a bus or a plane

A distant hallway filled with others who

So easily accepted that this was the best path

Out of wherever it was they started

We are all in it together then

Sharing success

Sharing defeat

Sharing spaces with people we hardly know

But somehow know better than the people

We'd known our whole lives before this

We learn the difference between the things that make us

And the things that unmake us

We learn the difference between the things that bind us

And the things that unbind us

We learn the difference between the things that move us

And the things that hold us still

It's such a short time that begins the path

And yet it stays with us for so long

I THOUGHT I KNEW

SEAPUP:

I thought I knew where I was going, but this isn't it at all.
Not sure it's bad though....

SEAMOM:

My dear, you must be lost to be found
broken to be mended
All alone before you can recognize your sisters

LETTING GO

The hardest part was letting go, jumping in and setting sail

It was the falling way it felt to jump, to plunge into dreams

The helpless way it felt to let go the certainty

Of grounded feet planted so still

Upon the shore I knew so well,

To set my sights upon this dream to discover

A world so vast so big so bright that

It contained mighty seas

That it contained this girl, the one I knew for the first time

Was the girl I was meant to be, had to be

The one who had this aching pain inside her heart to

Wander, to see the world out there that begins right here

With this one step

On this shore

I'd never thought I could actually see before

FATE

SEAPUP:

This isn't where they said I'd be.....

SEAMOM:

Oh child, did you not see what you signed?
Oh yes, the goddesses of chaos made you feel chosen
Made themselves sound like fate
With a design inspired by everything you are
Alas, you forgot to look before you leapt
You didn't make sure how it was written

You see,
All the mistakes down here
Are written in our own blood and tears

LUCK

I learned about luck one night

When two girls were each in a room filled with boys

Boys they saw every day,

One was fine, one wasn't

I learned that there are no safe spaces

That cannot be taken

No ways to tell which people will turn

No reliable management of risk

That can't be anticipated

Turned on its head

Planned for

Even luck runs out sometimes

YELLING INTO THE WIND

SEAPUP:

What happens when they try to tear me apart?
What happens when they succeed?

SEAMOM:

I wish the answer was more than nothing
I wish there was more to do than
Say the things that were done to us
Done around us
Done to our sisters
Maybe one day it will change
Maybe one day they'll have reason to fear the way they already do
Maybe one day our voices will change their fates
When they have changed ours
For now,
Yelling into the wind together is what we have

15

SHAPESHIFTING

They tried to make me something else at first

A barefoot beach bum doesn't turn into a sailor

As easily as one would think

Nor does she turn to a tinkerer

With any sort of ease at all

After years of toil, it just happened one day

my salty heart remained, the desire to

Be barefoot and bask in the sun did too

But a transformation took place

Surrounded by fish of sorts

Turning into some strange combination of

Tentacles and scales and lungs

SHAPESHIFTING

Unsure of what to breathe

When at last, I gasped new life

I realized the gift

I wasn't taught to sail or tinker

I had learned to transform

To live different lives

Submission to the goddess of chaos

Had been the price

CHANGED

SEAPUP:

> *Everyone back home says I've changed*

SEAMOM:

> *Tell them they have mispronounced*
> *"grown"*

TRADITION AND HERITAGE

Tradition? Heritage?

When I arrived, your traditions were

Hazing, drugs, harassment

Hurting us and denying that it

Should have hurt at all,

Saying that it wouldn't hurt

If we weren't so sensitive, weak, different

When I arrived, your traditions were

Separating us into smaller groups

All the easier for the taking of liberties

Not offered or consented to

They were discarding us when we were

SHAPESHIFTING

No longer of any use to you

When you assumed we would no longer

Be able to pretend to be like you

When I arrived, the separations were so

Much more than woman and man

So many finite places

Where it wasn't supposed to be

So what did we inherit? What became the

Heritage that we were meant to have?

We'll probably never really know

Those that came before had already been working

Building momentum for changing all the things

That arbitrarily stood in their way

Changing all the ways that others once stood

In the way of all those just trying to do the job

I inherited momentum

My tradition is to keep it going

SHARING THE WEIGHT

SEAPUP:

Is it always like this?

SEAMOM:

Not exactly.
It was different for me.
It was different for my seamothers
It will be different for your seapups
It will probably always
Seem like some kind of unbearable

Yet we bear it
Those of us who know that the trick to it is
sharing the weight

SOME MEN

Not all men

Are so afraid to lead us

Because of what they heard

Unsubstantiated

Accusations

Thrown about everywhere

Not all men

Are so accustomed to

Crossing boundaries

That they don't understand

Where they are

Not all men

See indications of

Boundaries coming near them

Without the slightest recognition

Not all men

Keep me up at night

Planning strategies to keep them at bay

Not all men

Stand in my way

Not all men

Even try to prevent the

Places we seek to thrive

TRUST

SEAPUP:

I don't know which one to trust.

SEAMOM:

None of us have ever known
All we can do is
Work with our whole heart
Rest before it breaks
Never let them get too close

Until we really know,
And even then, many hurt us

Our chances are better with the sharks

CAUTIONARY TALE

In the beginning I felt like a cautionary tale

What happens to little girls who think they're smart

Little girls who dare to dream of seeing things

All the things that made this world

I strived but failed a lot

Academics to athletics

Nothing was good enough

To be good, only

Good enough to pass

Little did I know that was all there was

That had to be done to get where I was going

SHAPESHIFTING

So long as it was evident that I was

Always trying, striving

Except for when it wasn't

Time came that it wasn't going to be enough

To be trying, striving, learning from mistakes

Time came when the simple makeup

Of my body was enough to cause disdain

There was no enough that could be and yet

I continued, persisted as is necessary when

Escape isn't an option, not even a whisper

Just when it all seemed like it was never

Going to get better, reprieve came in a strange form

It came in the form of replacement, rotation

Those who tried to tell me I would never be

Good enough to be even a little successful

Rotated out, and in wandered someone else

Someone who would wonder why things were

The way they were for everybody and then change it

Someone who would abide by the rules

As they were supposed to be more closely

And everything changed.

A cautionary tale against trying to be more

Became something else entirely

A cautionary tale of what can happen when

We simply try and persist and know

That this too shall pass

DOES IT REALLY GET BETTER?

SEAPUP:

Does it really get better?

SEAMOM:

Really
You learn that the biggest mistake you made
Was being new in a world with no patience

Somehow never seeing when the tables have turned

THE ROTATION

There's a beauty to the rotation

Of people in and out of our lives and work

There's a turnover here of people who

Spend their time in this one place with us

Then move on to the next adventure

There's a beauty to what they leave behind

The little ways they made things brighter

The little things they said or did that helped us

Get through another day in a dismal place

Of course, there too is a relief when

Those we do not miss will leave, taking

Their disappointment, disregard,

Disrespect along with them

Those we hope to be replaced by more

That we would miss, learn from, adore

We live with the memory

Ghosts that will haunt us

In the passages, in the workspaces

In the meetings they no longer speak in

The advice they are not around to give

More will come to take their place

Work alongside us, make us smile

We'll tell them about those who left

On it goes when we too must depart

When we become the remembered mate

Of someone standing on that deck

I MISS THEM

SEAPUP:

I miss them

SEAMOM:

Me too, honey, me too
They aren't really gone though
Not in this day and age
They are a message and some patience away

SEAPUP:

I'm glad they're gone

SEAMOM:

Me too, honey, me too
They aren't really gone though
Not in this day and age
Their legacy lives on
In all the things we'll never do

INDIFFERENT

When I first started you were indifferent to us

You barely noticed when seventeen of us died

From a warning shot directly in our side

Then came a day when they made YOU feel

That your safety wasn't so secure either

You saw that it didn't take drastic measures

On their end to make drastic effect on ours

When almost 3000 died in a matter of moments

That was when you remembered us

You remembered that we had a purpose beyond

Dying in foreign countries for just existing there

That we're only in those places to protect the

Interests and safety of those of you who stayed at home

You remembered and you celebrated us

You acted as if you had always cared

You continued this charade until the memory

Began to fade of what had happened on that day

When we asked for what you said we deserved

Sometimes you said yes, sometimes you said no

Sometimes you got mad at us for asking

Sometimes you saw an opportunity to swindle

Then after all the heartache and the PTSD

You just gave it back to them

Once you were indifferent again entirely

WERE YOU THERE?

SEAPUP:

Were you there when it happened?

SEAMOM:

Not exactly
I saw the smoke
Felt a panic for the things that could happen
Felt a panic that swept the whole country
Saw the shift take place
From unimportant
To our most precious commodity
Saw what happened to them after,
Those who took the brunt of it

The greatest lesson for us, though

HEATHER STEWART

Never underestimate your training
It is there for you on the bad days, when nothing else is

THE LITTLE THINGS

One summer, I was taught

The value of fixing the little things

That fix the bigger things

That keep the world I know still turning

Later, I realized the flaw in this

It isn't little things that break bigger things

Fixing little things only

Sets them back up to be broken again

And fixed again

And broken again

On and on it goes

Until someone comes along

And sees the bigger things,

Like climate and culture that

Are breaking everything, that

Leave little symptoms in their wake

For people like me to fix again

When we fix the little things

That break the big things

They just break again

When we fix the bigger things

That broke the little things

The whole system gets better

MENTAL TOUGHNESS

SEAPUP:

What's mental toughness?

SEAMOM:

A term they tried to supplant mental health with
So the public didn't fear the very thought
That we may not all be all together
That the way we live may unwind some
Mostly, made to shelter their ego under

After all
Who is worried about health
When they're tough?

A VAST EXPANSE

When at last I could reach out

A vast expanse lay before me

Sky and sea that met somewhere far away

Simply blending in shimmering blue

Salty air in the breeze out here,

The sun so high and warm

I never knew how much there was

Just beyond what I had always known

There was no way to stop or turn around now

To stop and try to be again that girl

Who sat upon a shore just wondering

What might be living in some other place

After seeing now what amazing life

Lay just beyond what I had always known

Wider than I had thought before,

Brighter than I had ever guessed

A whole world of things to do and see

Lay brilliantly before me

No going back, no turning 'round

No sitting still, no quieting down,

No room was left for all the rules that held me down before

FLYING

SEAPUP:

> *It feels like flying*

SEAMOM:

> *It really can*
> *The tumbles and the wind*
> *The lift and the buoyancy*
> *The safety net that doesn't feel needed*
>
> *Yet*

FREE

I sailed away from shores I'd known

Free from boy and girl, young and old

Just wandering along the mighty sea,

No one else's thought of what I'd be

No one's rules to change or roles to play or be again

Just open arms and open seas and striving, trying, doing

Just doing things I longed to do and seeing things

Just getting there and standing tall, just reaching out

Touching life, not asking anyone to let me do the things

I thought to do when all my life I'd thought of things

No longer pressured by the little things, mistakes I'd made

Or dreams I'd lost along the way before

Not pressured by the bigger things, held down below

Where someone thought I ought to go,

My thoughts, my dreams, this wondrous thing

Who brought me here not knowing

How I'd spread my wings,

Now that I was free of all the girls

They all thought I should want to be

SOARING

SEAPUP:

Why would you stay tethered here
When they taught you how to fly?

SEAMOM:

I flew
I flew so far for so long
That I came right back around again

You'll see, one day
The way a safety net such as this
Can make the surrender so much sweeter
When we give in to things like
Gravity and buoyancy

SEAPUP:

But how is that flying?

SEAMOM:

Baby, it's more like soaring

STANDBY TO STANDBY

Standby to standby

Hurry up and wait

Stand right here and make sure

Nothing significant happens

There's a sweet spot in the waiting

A daydream or conversation

A comment that grows to an inside joke

A story that gets passed along, getting bigger

Don't waste these precious moments

Waiting for the paint to dry

Waiting for a turn or a correcting word

Watching nothing happen

These precious moments between

Friends, colleagues, accomplices

These are the moments

That live the longest

BOREDOM

SEAPUP:

> *I'm bored.*

SEAMOM:

> *Shhhh.... you'll ruin it*

THE TELLING

There's a difference in the telling

Between those who know and

Those who need much more explanation

For those who know

Punchlines can be acronyms or titles

Jargon smooths it all out

The easier to get the point across

For those who need explanation

We may cut a few corners, not really

Explaining things as they are, giving

The relation to the point instead

If I said that a Turkish officer's crush

Led to my boss smoking on their bridge

It would need a little more explanation

For some, others would shrug and just say

That checks

Nothing Happened

SEAPUP:

Wait, how did that even happen?

SEAMOM:

It didn't, kid
You saw nothing
and
Nothing happened

But if something did happen,
It's best told
Once upon a time
In a land far, far away
Where sailors were doing sailor things

PERCEPTION

If perception is everything,

How do I manage

What someone else sees?

Believes?

Makes up in their heads?

If perception is everything,

How do I guard against

The things that are untrue

But cannot be easily disproven?

We all fall into the same trap of

Believing what we perceive of others

We all figure out our own way

We all wish it didn't have to be so

Maybe we all will learn one day

Remember that we have twisted

What is seen and what is known

In so many little ways along the way

Perception isn't all

Expectation helps

None of it is truly in our own control

It's more a matter of surrender

BECAUSE THEY CAN

SEAPUP:

Why do they talk about me like that?

SEAMOM:

Because they can

SEAPUP:

How do I make them stop?

SEAMOM:

You can't.
Well...
You can't just expect them to stop

There are some choices, but you aren't ready yet

SEAPUP:

How do I get ready?

SEAMOM:

When you are always seen working, learning, qualifying
When people ask you for advice on getting into programs
When your opinion matters
That is when you will be ready

SEAPUP:

What happens then?

SEAMOM:

A door opens and their opinion doesn't matter anymore

PERSPECTIVE

I held a scope one day

The scope through which they saw the world

A beautiful, majestic thing

Made of technology that feels ancient now

That stood larger than life as it was removed

From the place they lived, into my hands

So delicately lifted, brought to safety

In a place to bring it back to life

But I didn't get it then, maybe I never will

What looking at the world through a scope

Can do to perspective

Everything is somehow bigger and more intense

Without actually being bigger or more severe

It's all the same and yet different

They can see the same things

They can say the same things

But they may mean something different

Or they may just feel different

They saw it like shadows in a cave

Reality obscured by what they've always known

Curiosity like a cancer killing the ingenuity

That once made them great

And yet the scope doesn't change a thing

It refracts and reflects the image of the world just as it is

NO VISION

SEAPUP:

> *Why don't they see things the same?*

SEAMOM:

> *Because they have no vision, not anymore*

I FOUND A MAGICAL PLACE

Salty air, sea, and sky

In every direction

More stars than still reside

In most night skies

Gentle rocking to a

Lullaby of waves and wind

Where an engine somehow calms

Salty air, sea, and sky

In every direction

A sun brighter than anything

I've ever seen before

SHAPESHIFTING

Gentle rocking to the

Steady beat of a heart

Waking every nerve

More magical than any

Fantasy I've ever read

THE WONDER

SEAPUP:

I'm not sure I can ever leave this place

SEAMOM:

You're beginning to see it now
The wonder
That still lives here

It doesn't so much fade
As we eventually crave rest

BELIEVE IT OR NOT

Believe it or not

Women are not a hive mind

We do not all think alike

Even similarly

Believe it or not

Our experiences are different

Other things contribute

Race, ethnicity, background

Believe it or not

We don't always like each other

Even when we defend each other

SHAPESHIFTING

We aren't always catty either

Believe it or not

It's important to realize

It's better to back each other up

To hold each other in check

In our own little groupings

Than to leave each other exposed

To whims of male opinion

Particularly with cutthroat men

Who cut down everyone around them

Believe it or not

It's all too easy for them

To cut us down one by one

When we let things like promiscuity

Tone, attitude, assertiveness

Be used against us individually

Believe it or not

Just disparaging the idea

Of those traits as a negative

Evens the playing field a little

Allows us to be free of

The things they use to weaken us

Believe it or not

Helping each other,

Mentoring each other too

Helps the whole tide rise

ONLY A MOTHER

SEAPUP:

Is that why you're helping me?

SEAMOM:

A little
It's why we found each other here
It's why they can try to help but nothing ever works
They aren't subject to the rules they set upon you
So they have no idea how to bend them

Only a mother can show you that

PART TWO
SHELLBACK

a barnacled creature
having been on the sea long enough to know better
having joined the Court of King Neptune

NOT PEOPLE

People are exhausting

Wanting things

Needing things

Hearing the wrong things

Every time I open my mouth

Making me put on the right face

Smile at the dumbest things

Keep it together when I'm the one

That did the dumbest things

While getting lectured or reprimanded

While I'm lecturing or reprimanding them

People are exhausting

You, on the other hand,

Don't drain what I have left

Don't do things that require

For me to do things about them

Don't ask for things in this space

You just are and you only expect

For me to just be

Just be me

Not a version of me

Not a happy me

Not even a smart me

Just the mood I am in

The way that I feel

Without asking

Which leads to one beautiful conclusion

You are not people

EVERYONE LOVED YOU

SEAPUP:

    I spent all day putting on the face you told me to have

SEAMOM:

    And everyone loved you for it

SEAPUP:

    I didn't

UNIFORMITY

We've been given guidelines for

Colors on nails and lips and hair

Jewelry that can be worn

Locations for tattoos

How much and how little we can weigh

Even when and where to wear the things

That keep us warm or cool at night

But all of these things are up to interpretation

Which is not uniform, not at all similar

From place to place, or person to person

Or the communities that have become

Their own little ecosystems

So when navigating these murky waters

Remember that to find your sea legs

One must be willing to weather a bit

Of a storm in conflict at times

To find the way that gets heard

To stand up for others

To change the way things are interpreted

Never lose sight of improving, and be open

To the new interpretations of others

To the realities of shifting cultures

To the possibility that the way it's always been

Isn't the way that's best or that it always has to be

Changes are made to such things as guidelines

And standards and uniformity by those people

Who thought apart from the crowd

Who weren't afraid to ask why

Who weren't afraid to give a new perspective

That lent to a new interpretation

That acknowledged real shifts and struggles

That no one else saw or realized before

And improve it for those who came after

A SIMPLE QUESTION

SEAPUP:

I'm not sure I can affect a thing out here

SEAMOM:

Once upon a time,
At an all-hands call with a joint chief
One girl asked a simple question

And every single girl in the whole organization
Breathed a sigh of relief

It's never impossible
When phrased correctly
With the right audience

IN CHARGE

If people are people

Not always special

How do they know who knows the way?

It is hard to see on paper,

Impossible to simply test for

Hard to nurture, easy to kill

Sometimes

They've been waiting long enough

Have done this before

Can answer all the questions the right way

Someone had a feeling they might know

But then

Sometimes they can figure it out

Sometimes they can't

Sometimes they get us there

Sometimes we're close

Sometimes we're not

Sometimes we find ourselves

In unexpected places instead

Some places better, some worse

Sometimes they look at you,

With all the experience they feel you have

Say that it is your turn to get us there

Sometimes they know you have an idea

Sometimes they just hope you do

Eventually, when you've been

In charge long enough

You realize no one really knows the way

That's when we really learn the secret

Leadership is an art

One has the talent that needs to be nurtured

Or they don't

One will never know until they swim

Or they don't

READY

SEAPUP:

I don't think I'll ever be ready

SEAMOM:

I don't think anyone ever is

Ready and able to rise to occasion
Are not exactly the same either

SOME LESSONS LEARNED

How we stick out is just as

Important as how we fit in,

Smart and capable may be required but

They are only part of the puzzle

Interesting, fun, personality

Play a bigger role in being chosen for the team

A good attitude is indispensable

It's just a test, even when it isn't

There may not always be a failing answer

But there will be a consequence,

Sometimes good, sometimes bad

There is a balance between control and

Surrender that all good leaders must learn

Mistakes must be made for growth to take place

Good leadership is the nurturing of that growth

Without losing the group or the mission

Each person under your care is placed there

To learn, be nurtured, guided by you no matter

What your feelings about them are

Even if trading is an option, it's not leadership

There is so much more to do than

The path they have laid out for you

One assignment may come with great reward

Sacrificing dreams for it may come with great regret

The years you can do the job are so much shorter

Than the years that may be lived beyond it

Plan Accordingly

BE WARY

SEAMOM:

Be wary of those who only see one path for you

One can see the difference
Between the people who care about you
And
The people who care about themselves or the organization
It is found when you tell them your dreams

Whether they help you find a path to them
Or
Whether they tell you there is only one way to do the things

RULES OF THE GAME

Don't assume that just because we're all playing

The same game that we play by the same rules.

You don't get to choose the rules that apply to you

Things that shouldn't matter still do.

The sooner you figure your own way around it, the better you'll be.

The rules I began with are as follows:

Learn how to ask questions, yes or no can go awry.

Don't be defensive or argumentative, always have an opinion

Standing up is necessary but so is losing sometimes

Be important to leadership, but not indispensable,

Perception truly is absolutely everything

Extra duties should be important to the command,

Contributing and improving it even without understanding

There may be a filter for success, but getting through

Is never a guarantee

I learned in later circles that these very rules

Are not universal in nature, applying to some

A detriment at times to others,

That was when I learned the importance of

Women mentoring Women

Mentoring by any demographic

But not by demographic alone

That was when I realized the importance of

Learning rules that applied to others too

That rules can change over time even

For the same person, because we age

We get better, we are perceived anew

We can change the rules

So the rules change

So the game is played a little differently

And again begins the cycle I hadn't realized was evolving

NICE

SEAMOM:

Be nice, but don't be a nice girl
Don't mother them either

SEAPUP:

But......

SEAMOM:

It's not that time for you.
Just learn the rules they've made for you
How best to follow them
When to follow them
How to break them
When to break them

SEAPUP:

Shouldn't I always follow the rules?

SEAMOM:

Follow the ones they've written down, yes
But the unspoken rules are meant to be
Broken and rewritten
When the times feel right

SEA STORIES

There's an art to a great sea story

A certain special way for it to be told

Almost like a fairy tale, but not always so cautionary

A sea story is true

Mostly it's true

In the simple way it reveals a truth

Like the Odyssey of old

A sea story about Laestrygonians

Consuming all his men may be seen

As a fantastic myth made to entertain

Unless you know that sailors are often

Consumed by obsessions, leaving carnage

Today's sea stories may be mundane

When compared to the myths and legends

Recorded for posterity through the ages

But they are nevertheless the same truth

And they are nevertheless the same tale

Even when they aren't

When I tell you I was turned into a mermaid

By a goddess of chaos and cast into the depths

or

That King Neptune twice climbed aboard

My vessel and transformed us

or

That I was once Persephone

Some of you will say I'm just telling a sea story

But those who know will know

THE LIE

SEAMOM:

In every great story
There is the lie
That tells the truth

Given the limited vocabulary of those back home
We tend to hardly ever say anything real

Substitutions may get us there
Though they are never as much fun

We can shapeshift too many times
To be recognizable

So we tell the lie
That lets them see the truth

THE BITTER END

We can only make so much rope

We can only anchor ourselves

To the most precious things in life

With the thread we have to create it

The harder we hold onto it

The more it burns as it pulls away

The more it unravels between us

A decision must be made

Shall we continue to try to control

The way we connect to those around us

Watching the rope as it goes,

SHAPESHIFTING

Regardless of how tightly we grasp it

Watching the colors change as it

Progresses toward the bitter end,

Fearing the way it lashes out as it

Takes our anchor down to the bottom

Leaving us untethered, adrift

Shall we surrender our control

Let go and see if we have enough left

To reach the bottom and anchor us

To the place we long to be

Or protect ourselves from the

Way it whips off the ship, still untethered

Still adrift, but perhaps leaving us

Still intact as well

Broken bollards and chocks will only

Leave broken places where anchors once held

Unable to be replaced until the deck is repaired

Intact, they leave space for new anchors,

Perhaps longer rope next time,

Perhaps a chain next time,

Perhaps an anchor that can also be a life ring

Either way, one must have an anchor to be safe at sea

One must evaluate if it suits the ship and adapts to the tide

One must find a way to where they want to be

Find a way to stay there,

Whether adrift on their own

Or anchored to something precious

EVERYTHING WAS FINE

SEAPUP:

I don't understand what's happening
Everything was fine.
We were fine.
Happy, I thought
I was figuring life out and we were gonna...
I don't even know anymore

SEAMOM:

Very, very, very few of us
Make the connection you thought you had
Sometimes a second try is all you need at finding it

WISHED

I think I wished

Upon a star for you

That's just what

Whimsical little

Girls do

I must have

Wished for everything

I could never be

And then prayed

Upon every candle

In every church

I've ever seen

For the simple things

Of loving

Being loved

Happily

Forever

And yet l never

Saw you coming

BABY STEPS

SEAMOM:

Baby steps
Nothing is certain
Lightning may not strike twice
But sometimes we just felt a jolt
Not knowing where it came from

Sometimes we do

No matter where it started
Baby steps
To find out where it's going
Are far safer

UNDERSTANDING THE ANCIENTS

I understand now why the ancients

Told their stories with gods and monsters,

In myths that are at once true and story

It is far easier to understand the dangers

When personified than to simply

Call it what it is

Dragons and gods

Demons and heroes

Conversations in the afterlife

Nightmares, resentments,

Really the things we never said

Never wanted to hear out loud

SHAPESHIFTING

We become heroes fighting unbeatable odds

The scars made visible, representations of setbacks

The ruins of our lives become an acceptable price for glory

The fight at the climax remains the focus

Rather than the haunting feeling that we never

Did enough

Tried enough

Won enough

Were enough

MYTHS

SEAPUP:

So you think all the old myths were true?

SEAMOM:

My dear, I lived them

SEAPUP:

Sure, but they're older than you.....

SEAMOM:

Then you don't understand myths.
They are more true than histories
They happened then and are happening right now
They are happening to you
Just wait until you meet Persephone or mourn with Demeter
Too many of us have become Medusa

They were never false, they simply
Spoke truths we couldn't face at home
Or at sea

MISSED EXPECTATIONS

Pregnancy doesn't always result in a baby

Not every marriage lasts

Being the only girl doesn't reduce the drama

This is not a meritocracy

Higher rank doesn't mean less to do at all

And the good old boys are not all gone

There are ideas we have when we are young

There are things we feel must be

True but that seldom are

We do not live in the world we wish for

The status quo rarely changes

Into the way we wish it worked

There are only two options

Do our best to play the hand we're dealt

To let go of all our missed expectations

Or take these lies and make them true

WE COULDN'T STOP IT

SEAPUP:

Why does it have to be like this?

SEAMOM:

Because we couldn't stop it
Every unfortunate generation tries
To change it for the next
While the fortunate ones try
To keep it exactly the same

And on and on it will go

THEY SAID IT WAS LIKE A FAMILY

I thought of what we want a family to be

Imagined smiles and laughter, the ability

To lean on each other for support

To gain strength from each other as needed

They said it was like a family

They weren't exactly wrong

I just had to remember that families

Can be vastly different when it comes

To stress

To support

To neglect

To leaning on each other

To the abuses of power

They said it was like a family

They didn't say that it was like the family

That doesn't appreciate each other's efforts

To improving the family, or anything at all

That misuses the authority bestowed on it

By having favorites, whether appropriate or not

They said it was a like a family

They didn't say that it was like the family

That fights every holiday without boundaries

One that doesn't have boundaries in any regard

Where a niece gets groped by an uncle or displays

Inappropriate behavior to get his attention

Where siblings don't just bicker, but plan

New ways to hurt each other ever more

They said it was like a family

They say that a lot

Be careful what family you go to

THIS TOO SHALL PASS

SEAPUP:

Then who do you depend on?

SEAMOM:

Whoever supports you there
Will hold you up
But remember what you learned before

This too shall pass

PERSEPHONE

Sometimes starting in the sun

Nurturing growth around her

A girl is taken, convinced, deceived

To go to places unknown

Sometimes without telling a soul

She becomes Queen of the Underworld

And not like other girls anymore somehow

Praised for her darkness there, held for the way

She can get it all done there, ignoring

The homesickness that can make it all bleak

She forgets eventually, that there ever was a sun

That bathed her shoulder in light

She forgets eventually, that there ever was anything

That could be bright, or happy, or girly too

She forgets what girly is

She learns what it means in this place

She learns to hate all the things that girls like

She forgets that they will never respect her

No matter how little she is like other girls

When, at last, she sees Demeter again

Goddess of the Harvest, she remembers

That nurturing things to grow

That minimizing misery and death

These are girly things too.

Eventually she realizes

She doesn't have to be who they tell her to be

It isn't a dichotomy

She is the Queen of the Underworld

She is the Goddess of Spring

And they should fear her

DEMETER, PERSEPHONE, AND MELINOE

SEAMOM:

It's beautiful, growing into Demeter
Seeing Persephone grow, return
Seeing her bring forth Melinoe
Who will truly haunt them

Each of us
Can be any of the three
To anyone we meet

There are other options too

HER

The first time I saw her I didn't know who she was

I had no idea that this was a daughter of Artemis

I thought she was just a boss, like others before her

It actually had to be pointed out, this truth

Once others knew who she was, they quaked

Fearing the wrath that befell those who crossed her

Enraged by the justice she would bring them

But all we had to do was tell them that it was for *her*

Things just happened around her once everyone knew

She was a goddess that the disdain of those who may have

Called her bitch, unapproachable, cold, or mean did not touch

She was a huntress who did not give up her prey

Who attained dominance and never

Had to remind them of it

I saw another iteration of her some years later

I knew what she was that time by the air around her

By the way the men spoke to her,

That caution in their voices

By the way everyone made way for her

To enter a room, a cause

The venerated way they all spoke of her

I wanted to be like her, wanted to teach the other girls

To be like her though I don't think I ever achieved it

I know how she did it but never felt I mastered it myself

I learned that they mostly could not appreciate the majesty of *her*

If they hadn't seen a true iteration

Rather than the imitation that I presented

I wanted them to want it, most of them never did

They didn't understand that what made her great

Wasn't in helping the men, or anyone else

She rarely had to say anything at all to make one cower

Her greatness simply shown through all that she did

She was a reminder that they had to do something great

To actually be something great,

To get the veneration they wanted

Those around her who were also great found her to be valuable

Treated her as such, with deference and respect

The coward, pretender, loafer, or incompetent who had been

Convinced of a false greatness by unjust pride

Were emasculated by her presence

Always Look For Them

SEAMOM:

Always look for them
Artemis
Athena
Demeter
Persephone
Melinoe
Medusa
And so many more

They are all of us
In different stages of this experience

ALL MINE

It's my fault

It's always my fault

When it happens around me

There is no "I was just standing by"

There is no shifting of blame

Problems are solved by those who see them

Safety is outside of rank or authority

I'm not the problem, though

I can't be *the* problem

Or I'd definitely have a problem

The problem doesn't take ownership

SHAPESHIFTING

The problem can't grow from this

Won't grow from this

Is already as good as it is ever going to be

It's my responsibility

It's always my responsibility

When it happens around me

There is no "I was just standing by"

There is no shifting of blame

Whether success or failure comes

It's my responsibility

It's my consequence

For better or worse

It's my responsibility to make the process smooth

Slow is smooth, Smooth is fast

When it isn't smooth, it's my fault

When it is, we will all celebrate together

Because it's also my team

Because when it all belongs to me

It *all* belongs to me

OWNERSHIP

SEAMOM:

Ownership, like control
Must be metered by surrender
Can't be held too tightly
Can be suffocated under its own weight

It grows as it ascends,
Shrinks on the descent

Each of us must have some
To really make something

PRINCESS

Maybe she's the princess

Just a damsel in distress

Flitting from one mess to another

Making everything about her

Maybe you just want to make her less significant

Because her glow outshines every little

Thing you try to do

That she's cute or petite or sweet

Makes you rage on the inside

Never allows you to say anything significant

Always makes you the bad guy for saying

That she's the princess

That she's gorgeous or mean

Lets you rage on the outside

Insisting that all the benefits seen

Are simply a product of wanting her

Wanting to be near her

Wanting to think that one can get more

That someone is already getting more

Lets you just say this or that, especially

That she's the princess

The princess

Like a damsel in distress

The princess

Never the hero of her own story

The princess

Who only matters because of her relations

Why not

The princess

Saving herself

The princess

Learning to take the lead

The princess

Taking the throne now

These aren't the narratives you want

To give her when you call her this

These are the narratives she's creating

A PRINCESS OF HER OWN MAKING

SEAMOM:

I'm just gonna sit back and watch
While my little princess
Conquers all of it

I especially love the way
She took that pejorative
And made it her hallmark

She is a princess of her own making
Also a queen

UNLEARNING

Unlearning is a harder thing to do

Than adjusting the brain to a new

Piece of information

Unlearning takes more time

It takes precious realization

Mining the heart and mind for truth

That lays buried under perceptions

Learned identities, learned roles

Unlearning is realizing that I am not

Who they say I am, I never was

They are also not who they say they are

There is a person there between

What they believe themselves to be

What they allow me to perceive

What they cannot help but show

There is a person behind the disguise

Each of us wears, that knows

We don't actually have any idea what we are doing

We are all just trying to make it work

To make it through another day with

As little disaster as possible

Unlearning is realizing that the people

You respect are flawed, terrified people

Who once were someone else's

Disaster of a friend

Unintended responsibility

Horrible coworker

Mess of a manager

Unlearning is realizing that you aren't done yet

Growing to who you're going to be

Accepting that we are here to help the process

Accepting that maybe you're further along

Then you thought you'd ever be

I WISH I HAD KNOWN SOONER

SEAMOM:

I wish I had known sooner
That this was not the place I had thought it was
That all these people, those I was afraid to let see
All the little flaws
Were just people, but not just people
They were always flawed too
Probably more of a bad influence than I realized
Kids that didn't grow up so much,
That were still kids who got better at hiding it than others

MATURITY

There's a moment, a split second

When everything changes

Thoughts and feelings about trials gone by

Turn to panic or embarrassment

It's the moment when we realize

That we really were that young

That inexperienced, that naïve

That ill-prepared for the things that life would bring

It's the moment when we wonder if we were

This young, this much of a problem

This entitled, this rebellious

SHAPESHIFTING

This full of our own importance

There's a moment, a split second

That we don't even know is coming until it does

Then everything that came before changes

It happens again and again

Every change of station, position, importance

Comes with a new understanding of all the problems

That we may once have been

Those of us that recognize it worry

Those of us who don't aren't there yet

A part of me hates the moment when it comes

A part of me appreciates that I don't have to be that person anymore

MISTAKES

SEAMOM:

Don't relive my mistakes, honey
I'm gonna need you to come up with your very own
Along your very own way

FINDING HOME

I was a pigeon once

That pretended to have the majesty of an owl

I went to see a wizard once

That said he only knew the tempest

Who fed me possibilities

Who showed me wonders

Who took me places

In a swamp filled with bees

Busy little bees

Building hives

SHAPESHIFTING

All around a world unknown

To most of us

I convinced a genie once

That never quite granted our wishes

Who sent us where we had to go

Who chose what was best they said

Who agreed to send me to that place

In a swamp filled with bees

Busy little bees

Building hives

That felt like home

That comforted

That calmed

The panic of my heart

I was transformed into a bee once

That helped the swarm make their hives

Who tried to smooth out the process

Who kept track of their things

Who made a home

In a swamp filled with bees

HOME

SEAMOM:

One day, home is suddenly not
Where you come from anymore
Its more than feeling at home somewhere
But we don't really know it until asked

Where is home?

COLLECTED THINGS

We all have collected things

From those we've loved along the way

A scarf or a book bag that went around the world

With someone else already

That saw the same places

That make us feel bound to those who first held them

Photo books and Spider-men

Constellations that always share night sky

That always can be found when missing home

Bed sheets and ridiculous pajamas

T-shirts and hoodies

Sometimes things that also remind us

Of who we used to be, to remind us

Of who we still can be, who we try to be

Sometimes just carrying on habits

Of people we'd hate to disappoint

We all have collected

The memory of the people we get out of bed for

To keep us going when we're away

PACKING LIST

SEAMOM:

Deployment packing list:

All the things they tell you that you have to bring
A little something from everyone you just can't live without

IS IT JUST ME?

Does anyone else feel

Like maybe it was all a lie?

Maybe we weren't

Protecting our country

Instead spreading a

Different oppression?

Maybe we weren't

Saving people

Instead being a

Different villain?

Maybe we weren't

The most advanced

Instead clinging to a

Different level?

Maybe we weren't

The best of anything

Instead bringing the

Worst of everything ?

No? Just me?

Okay....

DIFFERENT CHOICES

SEAMOM:

At some point, most of us stop believing the lies
Sometimes we create lies of our own
To tell ourselves that we aren't monsters

When we really doubt it
We start making different choices
Forever embattled with those who never questioned
Whether we were doing what was right
Or whether this was what people believed kept them safe

HERITAGE

Am I ever truly a part of your Heritage

If you can decide to take my name away?

Heritage is spoken so highly of here

Stressed and distressing

Mentioned and shouted about

We hold traditions to know where we came from

They're supposed to show us where we are going

Then a name is changed

Erased

Shifted ever so slightly

Away from what it really meant

Are we to be grateful when

Who we are is changed by those on high?

Are we meant to celebrate when

We have been forced on a new path?

This isn't heritage, maybe it never was

This is a place where people have been before

Where people have lost themselves

Where people have found themselves

Who learned that maybe it isn't what we thought, maybe

Heritage isn't dictated by the system

That thinks they can change us

By changing our names or taking them away entirely

Heritage is dictated by the person

Who stood in my place before me

They aren't one kind of person who goes by one kind of name

Heritage is dictated by the person

Who stood in their place before them

And on and on until we arrive

At the first person who stood on a ship,

The ocean breeze in their hair

And thought that it was where they were meant to be

PART THREE
MERMAID

an enchanting sea creature; siren
attempting to call practices needed to existence
attempting to cull practices that need to go

THE PERSON STANDING NEXT TO THEM

SEAMOM:

You see, my dear,
Those on high think they dictate our actions
When most I have known are moved by
The person standing next to them
The person they would hate to disappoint
And
The person they know they will one day leave behind in this place

It has surprisingly little to do with
The edicts and decisions of those who believe they control us

I WAS JUST DOING MY JOB

I was just doing my job

Helping them envision

What could be in store

If they wanted it

Or not....

I was just doing my job

Finding ways around incompetence

Around leadership that

Led nowhere at all

Building roads and connections

To getting it done

I was just doing my job

Helping the unworthy

Who happened to work for me

Who happened to not have fallen

From the unworthy pedestal

I found them on

I was just doing my job

Delivering the bad news

Of the things I couldn't attain

For the worthy, yet underappreciated

Showing them the ridiculous

Things required for the accolade

They missed this time

I was just doing my job

Contributing to the mayhem

And the intrusion we provide

Into everyone else's business

Because it's better business for

Our own self-interests, well

Not all of our own, just those who

Make the big decisions

The big life-ruining decisions

The big country-ruining decisions

Whether that country is ours or not

But I was just doing my job

The job I thought I signed up for

That I increasingly felt was maybe not such

An honest day's work than I originally thought.

IT'S A CURSE

SEAMOM:

It's a curse sometimes
To do the things that you know you're supposed to do
Wondering which will keep you up at night

Fulfilling a role that you didn't believe in
Or
Intentionally failing it

Is it more important to say that I did what I was supposed to do
Performed my tasks as expertly as I could
Knowing that it did me no good at all
Even that it thwarted my own existence?

SHAPESHIFTING

Well, my dear,
When it's time for you to make these decisions
Know that neither choice will bring you comfort
For neither is right
We cannot refuse to do our job, once told what it is
And feel good about it
Neither can we actually do our job sometimes
And feel good about what the result we know it brings

Try to live with the outcome
I will greet you with a drink
Maybe a box of tissues
Or cookie dough
And we can regret it all together

AMBITION

Here lies the remains of my ambition

Salted, burned, and buried

So that I might move on

Without the haunting of ghosts that

Remind me of what I wanted once

I didn't strike the first blow

I never even wounded it

I merely removed the life support

That kept its unsteady breath

When it fell, I saw it

What it had done to me long ago

What it was doing to me then

The way it kept clutches in my heart

But I couldn't let go at first

I stayed with it, watching it breathe, thinking

It was a part of me that had been ripped out

But it wasn't, it was its own thing

Fed by others around me to make me think

That I wanted what they wanted for me

That I wanted to be what they wanted to say they made me

But I couldn't stay with it forever

I left it there, thinking that it would heal if

I just persisted down the road I was on

Heckled by those who knew me better

Warned to not let go by those who wanted the control

I left it there long enough that I realized

It had been a parasite

It had never been a part of me

It just fed off me, as did they

It should have been obvious

I could always dream of the accolade

But could never bring myself to do

What I knew it required

I had let go of the goal without even realizing it

Wishing for it despite the resistance of my soul

It would have been nice to have

Though not worth what it would have taken

From a heart not really in it

IF I'M BEING HONEST

SEAMOM:

If I'm being honest
I hadn't really nurtured it
It was unable to withstand the attack that befell it

Greater than the alphanumeric number assigned
Greater than the title I had worked so hard for

Were the things I got to do
The places I got to go
The difference I got to make
In a sometimes subtle way, in a brand new kind of place
Where not many people like me had ever been before

RIG THE SHIP FOR FEMALES

Rig the ship for females

Changes must be made, accommodations they say

Things cannot be the way they've always been

To make way for this nuisance, the inconvenience

To find a way for such a place to be habitable by

WOMEN

Change the ship, change yourselves,

Hide the unsavory side, they only want one thing

To get you into as much trouble as is humanly possible

Making false reports! They'll steal your jobs,

They'll lie about what you said,

Or the way you stood near them

They'll get pregnant and blame the honorable men!

Say this, not that, to avoid offending them!

How about this instead?

Let us make our own way, figuring how to amend

Practices that you do one way but may work for us another

In getting the exact same project or assignment done

All we really ask of you is to not stand in our way,

Not touch us or threaten to touch us without consent

Stay appropriately dressed in places we share

Let us be ourselves without extra condemnation and we

Will let you be you without extra condemnation and we

Will tell you when you've crossed the line as we expect

To also be informed of boundaries

We know that evil existed here before us

Some is bound to accompany us as well

But must we all punish each other for the evil

That most of us have no part of?

We know that some of you will see and some will

Even appreciate our presence when you find

That you rather like the little things that just happen

Like all your brethren improving hygiene

Like all your brethren staying fully clothed

Like the scent of lotions wafting through the passage

INTEGRATION

SEAMOM:

Integration is hard
None have ever gone flawlessly
But we are people too

I know, as do those who have walked this path already
That once you get used to us
You'll wonder how you ever lived without us

Just have patience and we can all get there

BEST OF THE BEST

Come on, you can't honestly

Believe that you are

The best of the best of the best

That the whole Defense is

One big spear and you are

The proverbial tip

Sure, you may gather some

Things hard to find, maybe

Pave the way with munitions

Even block well sometimes

But it's a far cry from doing

It all by yourself

No one is self-sustaining here

We couldn't breathe forever

Without relief from someone

You so quickly look down upon

It is a team effort every time

You are not the star player

You must know that

You make your job hardest

Being unbearable to be with

Driving friends away

Driving help away

Thinking all quake in fear of you

You hunt, quietly on the outskirts of connection

Watching and waiting and collecting

Information for that perfect chance

You lurk, seeking opportunity

Rather than creating it

Not so much preparing as awaiting

That moment when you can Strike

Disappointed when it doesn't come

Practicing for if it ever does

There's fear, but it's not what you think it is

NOT A REAPER

SEAMOM:

We may have feared some of you
Maybe on the old playgrounds
Like children fearing pedophiles
While you seem to think
All fear you like the reaper

No not a reaper, not to be feared as death
An inevitable part of life
But one who seeks to take advantage

IN THE PEOPLE TANK

Being in a people tank is surprisingly fun

Movement is so much more deliberate

Than resting on the water

The angle of the bow, whether up or down

Can provide its own entertainment

For those of us blessed with easy amusement

It's a delicate affair, such as tanks are

Keeping the balancing act going between

What we should breathe, and what's in the air

What we should drink, and what's in the water

The water itself, its disposition, displacement

Knowing the right amount of oxygen to share

There's a trust in the actions of each person

At each delicate station, performing just right

Which keeps the ratio of going under

And coming back up

Even when they can't be trusted for much else

There's a thrill in the moment, hearing the klaxon,

Feeling the shift beneath your feet, beginning to lean

Hearing the sound of the ballast changing

Counting the feet, feeling the pressure

Despite the anxious heart of being with people

I'd rather escape the presence of,

There was a release of pressure each time

I stood in a place where I had always been told I would

Never be allowed to be

I hope they get a hit of cortisol every time

They think about us being here

I hope they turn in their graves every time

We dive into the sea

MAGIC

SEAMOM:

There's a magic to everything
Something that makes it so much better
Than sitting in a cubicle somewhere
The key to every command is finding that magic

It's not always the same for everyone

SILENCED

If a woman screams beneath the ocean

And no one is around to hear it

Will anyone ever do anything about it?

I understand the answer to be no,

No one will hear, no one will act

Even when she's told them, over and over

Exactly what she had feared

Even when she produces pages upon pages

Written by their own hand

The things they want her to comply with

Her cries for help get drowned out by the storm

Of all the reports that must be made

And compiled

But nothing is DONE

So she screams against the storm

Until her voice is hoarse

Leaving her as silent as the mermaid

She was once so excited to become

TRUTH CAN BE SET FREE

SEAMOM:

We often feel like there's no point
When no one listens anyway
Not while we still wear the uniform
We can't be heard under the cacophony
Of papers fluttering

But later, when we are no longer able
To be threatened by them
Truth can be set free

DROWNED

I never felt so silenced as

When I worked to get fins

It wasn't just a single thing, or person, or storm

It was the battering of waves

The wake of an ocean liner

The constant streaming rain

That weakened my limbs

Made it hard to swim any further

Made it easy to be taken by the current

Made it possible to slip deeper

Than I ever thought I would

In the end

I drowned in my own ecosystem

OUR VOICES WILL BE THE STORM

SEAMOM:

> Still, when you have been wronged,
> Have the lungs for it, the support to keep you sane
> Scream as loud as you can
> For as long as you can
>
> One day our voices will be the storm

MOSTLY IT DOESN'T BOTHER US

Mostly it doesn't bother us

When you inventory and catalogue us

According to your preference

But when you lay out a plan to take what isn't yours

We all have bigger problems

When you conspire to make us comply

When you discuss force

These things are not consent considered

These things are not even consent requested

These things ignore that altogether

SHAPESHIFTING

When you take or talk of taking

That which wasn't freely given

That is when you have a problem with all the power

That you don't actually have in this world

That is when we have a problem with all the power

That you think you are entitled to

Did you think that we didn't all know that

The potential for lust and minuscule status in this world

Could make someone desire and discuss and plan

To possess a body that isn't theirs?

We walk among it every day

Every where

All the time

But you wrote it down

You shared it among you

You made it our problem

Then we all had bigger problems when your brethren

Came down with demands of reconciliation

That we contribute to building harmony when we did not

Build the discord that brought these brothers to us

We all had bigger problems when they decided

That it was time

To recreate the entire endeavor

By removing those among you

That made it all seem okay to talk of taking what isn't yours

REPEAT AFTER ME

SEAMOM:

Repeat after me

Nothing on a government computer is a secret
Nothing on a government computer is really gone forever
Nothing on a government computer is covered by privacy, Not like this

Anything written down is considered documented
Proving that it happened
That it was discussed

If you don't want it coming to the light
Don't write it down
Don't be surprised or hurt when it's used against you
Don't be surprised when others
Write down despicable things to use against all of us

HEATHER STEWART

Harassment is harassment
Even when you think they won't see it
Because they will
Especially when you saved it on a government computer

APEX PREDATORS

They all seem to think of themselves

As apex predators, but they aren't

They're just cannibals

Feasting on their own community

Wondering why there aren't enough of them

Condescending to other species about

Everything their small number can do

They never learn that

If you stop eating your own,

You wouldn't have to be so busy

PREY

SEAMOM:

You may be a predator
But you are also someone's prey

We are all hunters
We are all the hunted

Pretending to stand alone
At the top of the food chain
Is a delusion that makes us
Vulnerable

BETRAYAL

There is a time and a place

Where a simple error

In the performance of one's duties

Feels like a betrayal

A warning to a supervisor

Of a thing done

Or trouble that may be yet to come

A missed notice

Of a happening

Or sorrow that may be yet to come

An unwanted action

Of a rejected title

Or distress that may be yet to come

Things that helped us on the surface

Things that created problems under water

In a world I don't think I ever understood

I'm sorry for the damage I've caused

I'M SORRY

SEAMOM:

I'm sorry
I'm sorry
I'm sorry

For some things, I will never
Be able to apologize enough
But it's never to those who think they're entitled to it

Learning to apologize
To those who do deserve it
Is one of the most important lessons

TO THE CONSEQUENCES OF MY GOOD INTENTIONS

You certainly paved a road

Where it was going, I didn't want to know

Maybe I didn't always think you through

Maybe I didn't always prepare enough

Maybe I didn't always get it right

I believed in the beginning

That it was better to take a chance on a dream

Than to wish it had happened to me

And I believed it

Until you showed up

SHAPESHIFTING

I learned somewhere in the middle

That it was better to get it done

Than to make sure it was perfect

And I believed it

Until you showed up

I forgot somewhere in the end

That it was better to fight and lose

Than it was to let the fight drift by me

And I believed it

Until you showed up

I thought I knew some things

How the world worked

How this place worked

How I might be perceived or received here

I thought I could step forward confidently

Things may not always bend to my will but

I could affect something somewhere

Until you showed up

You didn't always come in and smash my toys

You didn't always come in and smash my dreams

But then it felt like a game of yours

It felt like I'd have nothing you wouldn't destroy

You certainly paved a road

Where it was going, I didn't want to know

I could stay and watch everything continue to fall apart

Or leave and maybe keep my soul

So I left you there, in the destruction you wrought

And I only think about you when I wonder to myself

How have I not always lived the way I do now

Basking in the sun, serene and comfortable

Far away from everything I thought I was meant to do

WHEN TO LEAVE

SEAMOM:

Knowing when to leave a relationship
Is an important thing to learn
Be it with people
Or with organizations

I decided to leave when it was clear
That no matter how much good I was trying to do
Things were only getting worse
For all of us, it seemed

Of course, I did learn since then
That I did a little good
Here and there
For my children in the sea

CONFESSION OF A MERMAID IN RECOVERY

I thought you were my everything

I thought I wouldn't know who I was without you

Maybe that was true for a while

But you turned on me

You took everything that brought the slightest bit of comfort

Everything I thought I needed from you

You tore it apart right in front of me

You trod it under foot until it was nothing

Until I felt nothing

Lost the sense of who I had always been until you

Somehow it set me free

Free to stop the shift

To turn, not into the shape of your mold

Not back into what I was before

It set me free to stop and think

About who I could want to be next

To sever the tie that bound me to you

And everything that has to do with you

Even what once was grand

About this shapeshifting life

I WAS GONE BEFORE
I LEFT

SEAMOM:

> I always thought I would miss it
> I was afraid of that
>
> I learned that everyone who would be
> In the after with me
> Were also afraid of that
>
> It turns out, when you leave
> At the right time for you
> There can be nothing left to miss
>
> I was gone before I left

RESUSCITATION

In some ways, I died a mermaid.

Gills speared by the things I loved the most

There was a failing of heart, a last

Incomplete transformation

Gills and fins and lungs, straining

To breathe in the place I was

Supposed to call a home

The place they said had the best

Camaraderie, that was supposed to

Have the best loyalty that I could never find

Mid-transformation, halfway to what

I was supposed to be, it all came to an end

SHAPESHIFTING

I found myself flailing in the deep

Unsure of where I was going

Unable to breathe through gills I thought had grown

I reached for help, needing resuscitation,

And washed ashore on a beach again

Brought back to life by the breeze and sun

Barefoot and basking in the light again

With all the freedom found of

Knowing how to be so many things

Knowing exactly what I want to be this time

DO NOT FEAR THIS CHANGE

SEAMOM:

So many get to this point and fear it
But leaving this relationship
Especially when it has become so toxic
When your very soul denies that this is where
You need to be to breathe
Do not fear this change

Things may be unknown
They may not even be what you wished or thought they were
But breathe the freedom that was forgotten
That was sacrificed
To offer a service that few truly recognize
It's a freedom that knows
You have already done more than most
To secure a better future for far more than yourself

I WAS NEVER ENOUGH FOR THEM

I was never enough for them, I didn't have to be,

Because I chose you every time there was a choice

Not contracts veiled with choice,

That was when I chose you

Not a minute today veiling an hour tomorrow,

But real time for us instead

That was when I chose you

I tried to make them believe that I chose them

I tried to convince myself it's what we're supposed to do

Choose them, those who pay us,

Those who promote, advance us

But I chose you

I tried to show them I was still worth it

Worth something to them even when

I would never really choose them

I wanted the pay, to advance

But I couldn't choose them

And they knew it, they knew it

When I chose you

I wish you would believe me

That you could see through the

Veils that were never choices

That you knew that I always bargained

With them for you, for time with you

That even though they took me away

I always chose you

I wish you could see that though

Today was more sure than tomorrow

I bet on it over and over again

I bet on a future where we have

More of everything and that was

HEATHER STEWART

Choosing you, even when I couldn't be

Immediately with you

I chose today, instead of yesterday

When yesterday was today

And seeing through the veil

Got more of you, more of what

I was choosing

Which was always you

CHOOSE THEM

SEAMOM:

> When someone really shares their life with you
> Choose them
> Every time there is a choice
> This place, this organization
> Is made to chew you up and spit you out
> They will not be there for you in the end
>
> The relationships made
> Whether friends, chosen family
> Intimate partners
> That is what we stand to take with us when we leave
>
> Take as much of it as you can

I WAS A SHAPESHIFTER

Traveling the world, seeing the wonder

Learning the lessons along the way

Of what it may mean to teach, to change,

To motivate, to be patriotic, to fight for one's country

To invest in a future we are never certain of

To see it all fall down around us sometimes

To be disappointed and weighed down by it

To also be proud of and uplifted by it

For a little over twenty years is an awfully long time

To be uncertain of where I will be when it all ends

To devote to something I knew wouldn't last

To not be sure I am living my own life

To not really take care of the people

Who are going to be here when it all ends

And they were and they weren't

Shifting causes shifts

The world never stays the same

The lessons come hard learned

Regret multiplies at times

Was it all worth it? They ask

Maybe it was and maybe it wasn't

Maybe it's too soon to tell

Milton Keynes UK
Ingram Content Group UK Ltd.
UKHW021008160924
448404UK00013B/764